MW01601973

IN

MY

FATHER'S HOUSE

A Revelation of Heaven

By Romel Duane Moore Sr.
Prayer Changes Things Publishing

In my Father's house

Prayer Changes Things (PCT) Publishing
7551 Kingsport Road
Indianapolis, Indiana 46256

Scripture quotations are from the King James Version of the Bible, unless otherwise noted.

Cover design by Jan Taylor

Printed in the United States of America.

Edited by Margaret Mejia

ISBN 13: 978-1537039053
ISBN 10: 1537039059

The name satan is intentionally not capitalized.

In my Father's house

TABLE OF CONTENTS

DEDICATION

This book is dedicated to the memory of a great matriarch, my Grandmother, Daisy Lee Satchell. There isn't a day that passes where I don't miss her humor, smile, and wisdom.

INTRODUCTION

John 8:32 says, "And ye shall know the truth, and the truth shall make you free." Freedom is connected to knowledge, knowledge of the truth. God does not desire His children to be ignorant concerning any area of their life, especially His Word. There are many untrue beliefs about Heaven and we must understand that a half-truth is a whole lie. It is imperative that we study to show ourselves approved unto God and rightly divide His Word, (***2Timothy 2:15***) in order for truth to prevail. God's Word is light, and it keeps us from the darkness of ignorance. *In My Father's House, A Revelation of Heaven* examines the Scriptures pertaining to Heaven and offers insight that will set one free from past doctrines of error and untrue realities concerning the Believer's expectations after death.

1

HOUSE OF GOD

"In my Father's house are many mansions: if it were not so, I would have told you. I go to prepare a place for you."

John 14:2

It is the desire of every Christian to see the Lord after leaving this world. Jesus' death, burial, and resurrection are the guarantee to every Believer of this truth. Before the Lord had the Last Supper with His disciples, He had an intimate conversation with them concerning God's plans for them and His plans for every future Christian. His Words in *John 14:2* are some of His most memorable ones. We have taken Jesus' Words to be our promise of a new mansion once we make it to Heaven. A little study of the Scriptures will unveil that Jesus was talking about something else.

The word translated *mansion* in this passage means, *rooms, residence, abode or a dwelling places.*[1] The same word is used further down in verse 23 of the same chapter where Jesus said, *"...and we will come unto him, and make our abode with him."* The translators of the King James Version of the Bible chose to use *mansion* instead of *room, abode, or a dwelling place.* It would be safe to read **John 14:2** this way, *"In my Father's house are many rooms..."* This Scripture is the only place the word *mansion* is translated from the Greek word *mone (*pronounced *mŏnē),* and it is the only time *mansion* is used in the Bible.[2] Jesus said He would prepare a place not a mansion. Most bible translations translate this word as room or dwelling place.

2 Timothy 2:15 says, *"Study to shew thyself approved unto God, a workman that needeth not to be ashamed, rightly dividing the word of truth."* God's Word is truth and He has given us His Spirit of truth. God does not desire for us to misunderstand any part of His Word because we are supposed to walk in truth. The pathway to truth, often entails exposing the lie. Jesus was not telling His disciples *in God's house "are many mansions."* He was about to depart to prepare *the disciples' dwelling place, room or abode.* Jesus was a carpenter on Earth, not in Heaven. Let us look at what Jesus did not say. He did not say, "I*n*

Heaven are many dwelling places." He said, *"In my Father's house* are many dwelling places."

The Father's House

We assume Jesus meant Heaven when He said, *"In my Father's house."* The Bible always interprets the Bible. We cannot take one isolated Scripture and make a doctrine from that Scripture. Let us look at what the rest of the Scriptures say concerning, *the Father's house.* **Hebrews 10:21** says, *"And having an high priest over the house of God."* **1Timothy 3:15** reads, *"...thou mayest know how thou oughtest to behave thyself in the house of God, which is the church of the living God, the pillar and ground of the truth."* **Hebrews 3:6** records, *"But Christ as a son over his own house, whose house are we, if we hold fast the confidence and the rejoicing of the hope firm unto the end."* **1Peter 2:5** says, *"Ye also, as lively stones, are built up a spiritual house, an holy priesthood, to offer up spiritual sacrifices, acceptable to God by Jesus Christ."* **Galatians 6:10** reads, *"As we have therefore opportunity, let us do good unto all men, especially unto them who are of the household of faith."* **1Peter 4:17** instructs us, *"For the time is come that judgment must begin at the house of*

God: and if it first begin at us, what shall the end be of them that obey not the gospel of God?" **Ephesians 2:19-22** reads:

Now therefore ye are no more strangers and foreigners, but fellowcitizens with the saints, and of the household of God;

And are built upon the foundation of the apostles and prophets, Jesus Christ himself being the chief corner stone;

In whom all the building fitly framed together growth unto a holy temple in the Lord:

In whom ye also are builded together for an habitation of God through the Spirit.

As we look at all of the New Testament, we find the definition of *the Father's house*. Jesus is the High Priest of God's house and the Chief Cornerstone. The *house of God* is the Church of the Living God, the city of God, the pillar and ground of truth. Christians are lively stones that make up God's *spiritual house*, of which we are the holy priesthood. We are to do good to all men, especially those who are of the *household of faith*. God's judgment first begins in the *house of God*. We are no more strangers, but fellow-citizens of the *household of God*, who are the holy temple in the Lord. The Bible concludes that the Church, who is the Body of Christ and all Christians universal, are the house of God. We are God's habitation, His building, and His city. God does not dwell in brick, stone, wood, drywall, institutions or denominations. God lives in man.

Temple of God

"...for ye are the temple of the living God; as God hath said, I will dwell in them, and walk in them; and I will be their God,   and they shall be my people."

2Corinthians 6:16

Jesus said, *"In my Father's house are many (dwelling places)..."* The Father's house is also God's temple. The above Scripture states that we are *the temple of the living God*, and He dwells in us, and walks in us. **John 2:19** records the conversation Jesus had with the Jews where He stated, "...Destroy this temple, and in three days I will raise it up." The Jews believed He was referring to Herod's Temple when in reality He was speaking of His Body as The Temple. **1 Corinthians 3:16-17** reads,

"Know ye not that ye are the temple of God, and that the Spirit of God dwelleth in you?

10

In my Father's house

If any man defile the temple of God, him shall God destroy; for the temple of God is holy, which temple ye are."

There is no doubt that we are the temple of God, and when we come together collectively, we make up His household. We are temples, and individual dwelling places for God, and we are His temple and dwelling place universally. Individually, we are a small house, and collectively, we are a great house. Jesus said, "In my Father's house are many (dwelling places)…" because together we make up *the Father's house,* while many individuals are its members. Within the Body of Christ, are millions of Christians. We are the many *mansions* of whom Jesus was speaking. A local Church has one building, but many members worshipping within the building. Together we are *the Father's house*, and individually, we make up the many *dwelling places*. Christ was not speaking of a distant place that we will one day experience. He was speaking concerning a reality that His death, burial, and resurrection would bring to pass.

Purpose of the Cross

"... I go to prepare a place for you."

John 14:2

Heaven is so awesome that words cannot describe it. If a mansion is sufficient for all the pain and suffering we must encounter for representing Christ in this life, then something is seriously wrong. I do not believe God is in Heaven building us a big house. Heaven is so splendid that the last place we will want to be is inside another house. The Bible says very little about Heaven other than it is a place where God and Angels dwell. We are going to take a journey through the popular passages we believe describe Heaven and find out the truth.

Jesus said that He was leaving to prepare a place for us. We understand now, the place He is preparing is not a *mansion*, but a *dwelling place*. What *dwelling place* is He preparing for us? Man was disconnected from God because of Adam's sin. Jesus' death atoned for our sins and prepared the way for us to be born again. The place Jesus is preparing for us, is the place of the regenerated

12

spirit. It is our born-again spirit that is redeemed and made in the image and likeness of God. It is the born-again spirit that is able to enter the Presence of God. Calvary prepared the place of fellowship for us to be able to commune with God again. If we did not receive new spirits, God would not be able to dwell inside of us. Christ made a way for our spirits to be renewed so that God could take up residence in us.

Jesus ended the conversation by saying, *"...that where I am, there ye may be also."* He did not say, *"where I am going."* But He said that where He was at the very moment, we will be also. Where was Jesus that we will be able to join Him? Jesus was in perfect communion with God. He had access to His Father. Jesus' death, burial, and resurrection opened the door for us to be where He was: in relationship with Father God. Adam sinned and caused all of humanity to fall from our original place and position in God. Jesus came to seek and save that which was lost. His work at Calvary redeemed and restored man back to our original place and position. *Ephesians 2:6* says, *"And hath raised us up together, and made us sit together in heavenly places in Christ Jesus."* *Romans 8:17* states, *"And if children, then heirs, heirs of God, and*

13

joint-heirs with Christ; if so be that we suffer with him, that we may be also glorified together."

In Christ

". . . where I am, there ye may be also."

John 14:3

We are many members who belong to one body (*1Corinthians 12:20*), the Body of Christ. Jesus' death, burial, and resurrection purchased all we have in God as Christians. Here is a list of Scriptures detailing what we have received *in Christ* because Jesus said, *"...where He is, we will be also."*

"Being justified freely by his grace through the redemption that is in Christ Jesus."

Romans 3:24

"For the law of the Spirit of life in Christ Jesus hath made me free from the law of sin and death."

Romans 8:2

"Therefore if any man be in Christ, he is a new creature; old things are passed away; behold, all things are become new."

14

In my Father's house

2Corinthians 5:17

"For ye are all the children of God by faith in Christ Jesus.

For as many of you as have been baptized into Christ have put on Christ.

There is neither Jew nor Greek, there is neither bond nor free, there is neither male nor female: for ye are all one in Christ Jesus."

Galatians 3:26-28

"Blessed be the God and Father of our Lord Jesus Christ, who hath blessed us with all spiritual blessings in heavenly places in Christ."

Ephesians 1:3

"For we are his workmanship, created in Christ Jesus unto good works, which God hath before ordained that we should walk in them."

Ephesians 2:10

"But now in Christ Jesus ye who sometimes were far off are made nigh by the blood of Christ."

Ephesians 2:13

"Now thanks be unto God, which always causeth us to triumph in Christ, and maketh manifest the savour of his knowledge by us in every place."

2 Corinthians 2:14

To wit, that God was in Christ, reconciling the world unto himself, not imputing their trespasses unto them; and hath committed unto us the word of reconciliation."

2 Corinthians 5:19

2

HEAVEN ON EARTH

"Thy kingdom come, Thy will be done in earth, as it is in heaven."
Matthew 6:10

Leaders in the Church teach the people that Heaven is our goal and that Heaven is where we want to make it to and what we desire as home after this life. They've taught the masses that if we can just make it through this life, Heaven, angels, God's Presence, streets of gold, pearly gates, and mansions are waiting on the other side. These teachings have produced a spirit of escapism. This is absolutely the opposite of what the Scriptures teach. The Christian goal isn't trying to make it to Heaven, but Heaven making it to Earth. Jesus taught us to pray, "Thy kingdom come. Thy will be done in earth, as it is in heaven." Our focus is supposed to be accessing Heaven on Earth not the other way around. We aren't supposed to be trying to get to Heaven because Heaven is trying to get to us. The purpose of Passover (Jesus' death and resurrection) and Pentecost (the

17

outpouring of God's Spirit) was to bring Heaven back to Earth like it was before man's Fall in the Garden of Eden.

We are so busy looking for His Coming, we've forgotten about His Presence. The Believer spends all his time praying for God's Presence, praying for God's blessings, praying for God's Kingdom, praying for God's deliverance, praying for God's mind when the truth is we already have His Presence, His Kingdom, His deliverance, His blessings, and His mind. Therefore, we should be praying *from* it, not *for* it; Praying from God's Presence because He lives in us, not for it, as if we are not born again. Praying from the Kingdom instead of praying for the Kingdom, as if we are strangers; Praying from God's blessings instead of praying for the blessings, as if He hasn't already blessed us with all spiritual blessings; Praying from the mind of Christ instead of for the mind of Christ, as if the Bible doesn't state, "But we have the mind of Christ." *1Corinthians 2:16b*

It's absolutely amazing how God's people have missed this truth. We are the Body of Christ. In order for His actual Body to be in the Earth, He must be present and if He is present, His Spirit is present, His Presence is present, His will is present, His mind is present, His Kingdom is present, His blessings are present, and His power is present. The Church acts powerless because we spend all our time and energy begging God for what He has already supplied!

Streets of Gold

"...and the street of the city was pure gold, as it were transparent glass."

Revelation 21:21

We were taught in Sunday School, Bible Study, and Sunday Service that Heaven had streets of gold. However, there is no such passage that states that in the Bible. The only Scripture that record streets of gold, is the above Scripture of *Revelation 21:21.* It never says Heaven has streets of gold. It records the city called New Jerusalem has streets of gold. Heaven is not New Jerusalem and New Jerusalem is not Heaven. If we take a quick look at this passage we will discover exactly what and who God was referring to.

19

In my Father's house

Revelation 21: 9-10 says,

"And there came unto me one of the seven angels which had the seven vials full of the seven last plagues, and talked with me, saying, Come hither, I will show thee the bride, the Lamb's wife. And he carried me away in the spirit to a great and high mountain, and shewed me that great city, the holy Jerusalem, descending out of heaven from God."

We have been taught and we sang songs about making it to Heaven where the streets are pure gold. We never went and checked to see if it was true. Apostle John said that one of the seven angels showed him the Bride, the Lamb's Wife and then he was carried away in the spirit to a great and high mountain and was shown a great city also called Holy Jerusalem. John then said this city descended out of Heaven. It was the city, Holy Jerusalem that had streets of gold, not Heaven and this city came down from Heaven. Much of the Book of Revelation is misunderstood because it is not read properly and it is usually interpreted literally. However, the Book of Revelation is a book of signification and representation. There isn't one verse that's says Heaven has streets of gold. John was shown a prophetic picture of the Church of Jesus Christ. Let's look a little closer at **Revelation 21:2-3,**

"And I John saw the holy city, new Jerusalem, coming down from God out of Heaven, prepared as a bride adorned for her husband.

And I heard a great voice out of heaven saying, Behold, the tabernacle of God is with men and he will dwell with them, and they shall be his people, and God himself shall be with them, and be their God."

God was speaking concerning His Church and called it a "bride adorned for her husband," "new Jerusalem," and "that great city." God was describing the Church of Jesus Christ. The Church is Christ's Bride. The Church is a city of light set upon a hill. The 21st Chapter of Revelation is a prophetic description of the Body of Christ. The foundation of 12 jewels; the pearly gates; the city; and the streets of gold, and measurement of the city, all give insight to the purpose of the Church.

Now that we understand that the streets of gold, are not the streets in Heaven, but Body of Christ, let's break it down all the way. Gold represents divinity, in the Bible. Peter said that our faith would be tried in the fire until it came out as pure gold (*1Peter 1:7*). So when we walk by faith and not by sight, we are walking on streets of gold because the steps of a good man are ordered by the Lord (*Psalm 37:23*). When the people of God mature and learn to walk by faith (that's been tried in the fire like gold) they are walking on streets of gold because their path and destiny is God-ordained.

Apostolic and Prophetic Foundation

"And the wall of the city had twelve foundations and in them the name of the twelve apostles of the Lamb."

Revelation 21: 14

This prophetic picture of the Church had walls which had twelve foundations and in each foundation was a name of one of the twelve apostles of Christ. Paul wrote that the Church was built upon the foundation of the apostles and prophets with Jesus Christ, the Chief Cornerstone (***Ephesians 2:20***). The foundation is the first part of any construction. The Old Testament is mostly written by prophets and the New Testament is predominantly written by apostles. Their words and their ministry is our foundation. The foundation of any building is the most important part of the structure. God made sure the foundation of His Church had no cracks because unlike man made foundations, the Church's foundation is laid with precious stones.

Twelve Precious Stones

"And the foundations of the wall of the city were garnished with all manner of precious stones. The first foundation was jasper; the second, sapphire; the third, a chalcedony; the fourth, an emerald.

The filfth, sardonyx; the sixth, sardius; the seventh, chrysolyte; the eighth, beryl; the ninth, a topaz; the tenth, a chrysopraus; the eleventh, a jacinth; the twelfth, an amethyst."

Revelation 21: 19-20

Twelve is the number of Apostolic Government. Twelve hours govern the day and twelve hours govern the night. Twelve months in the year govern the season. Twelve vertebrae of the spine govern the nervous system. Twelve inches in a ruler govern measurements. Twelve apostles governed God's Kingdom on Earth. The New Jerusalem had twelve precious stones as its foundation. Jesus is the Chief Cornerstone and the Church is built upon the foundation of apostles and prophets.

The Bible says that we should be wise builders and count the cost before we build a house (*Luke 14:28*). Building takes wisdom and the most important part of any structure is its foundation. In God's wisdom, He came down and became the Chief Cornerstone. *Proverbs 8:11* says, *"For wisdom is better than rubies; and all things that may be desired are not to be compared to it."* God uses precious stones to represent His wisdom. Paul talked about the manifold wisdom of God. *Manifold* is from the Greek word *poikilos* meaning *particolored* or *many colored.* Why is God's wisdom many colored? The reason God's wisdom is many colored is because His wisdom is precious stones and precious stones come in many colors. Therefore, the foundation of the New Jerusalem is built by the wisdom of God and is represented by twelve precious stones.

Manifold Wisdom of God

"If any of you lack wisdom, let him ask of God, that giveth to all men liberally, and upbraideth not, and it shall be given him."
                                                                James 1:5

In ancient times before we had banks and safes for storing money and expensive items, women would braid their hair and put it in an "updo" (upbraid it). As a security measure, they would place their precious stones deep inside their braided hair that was in an "updo." In case they were robbed, the thief would not think to look inside the woman's hair. God said that if any of you lack wisdom (represented by precious stones), let him ask of God Who gives wisdom liberally and does not upbraid it. God doesn't want to hide wisdom from His people, as women hid jewels in their braided hair. We are not thieves looking to forcefully or illegally take from God, but we are bone of His bone and flesh of His flesh and we have a covenant right to the manifold - many colored precious stones of God's wisdom. Ask and it shall be given. God is saying that when we ask Him for wisdom, He will let His hair down and let every ruby, sapphire, diamond, pearl, carbuncle, topaz, emerald, and jasper fall for us to know, understand, and use to help build His Church.

The Bride Adorned

"I will greatly rejoice in the Lord, my soul shall be joyful in my God; for he hath clothed me with the garments of salvation, he hath covered me with the robe of righteousness, as a bridegroom decketh himself with ornaments, and as a bride adorneth herself with her jewels."

Isaiah 61:10

God shall prepare Israel and adorn her as His wife with precious ornaments and jewels. It was and is still an Eastern custom for the husband to adorn his new wife with gold and precious jewels. *Genesis 24:15-61* records how Abraham sent his head servant to find a wife for his son Isaac. His servant found Rebekah watering the camels at the well. After explaining to Rebekah that he is looking for a wife for his master's son, and she accepts to be Isaac's wife, the head servant adorns Rebekah with gold and precious jewels as a symbol that she has entered into a betrothal. Abraham represents Father God and his head servant is a picture of God's Spirit sent to the Earth, on the day of Pentecost, for the sole purpose of finding Christ a Bride. Every Believer who accepts the Spirit's invitation is adorned with God's wisdom of precious stones, signifying they are betrothed to the Lord Jesus Christ.

The twelve precious jewels in the City, the New Jerusalem, represent this truth. The New Jerusalem is the Church and comes out of Heaven as a Bride prepared for her Groom. We are the Bride of Christ and the twelve foundations of precious stones in the New Jerusalem represent the adorning of precious stones, the decorating of God's manifold-many colored wisdom on Christ's Bride signifying that we are bone of His bone and flesh of His flesh and bought by the Blood of the Lamb!

God's River

"And he showed me a pure river of water of life, clear as crystal, proceeding out of the throne of God and of the Lamb."

Revelation 22: 1

Now that we understand that the city isn't a city, we understand that the river isn't a river. Jesus said out of our bellies would flow rivers of living waters, speaking of the Presence of the Holy Spirit (*John 7:38*). *Genesis 2:10*, states that a river flowed from Eden into the Garden and parted into four heads into the rest of the Earth. The Presence of the Holy Spirit in the Believer's life causes the Believer to flow and moistens our life and walk. We are all born into sin and sin makes our lives dry, parched, and cursed. The Presence of God's Spirit is like life-giving water, a river of life: watering, nourishing, feeding, and giving health to every area of our lives. Every example the Bible uses to represent the Holy Spirit has moisture: olive oil, clouds, rain, rivers, and new wine. The anointing oil of the Spirit, the cloud and rain of the Spirit, the river of the Spirit, and the new wine of the Spirit all signify the presence of moisture in the Believer's life.

The Church of God, the Bride of Christ, the Body of Christ is the only Entity on Earth who has this river which flows from God's throne. God has delegated access to His river only to the Bride of Christ. Everything we have from God is for the benefit of this dying world. We have God's river so we can water those who are dying from sins cursed, dry life. The saving grace of God is the only thing which can alter man's famine of hopelessness, sickness, and despair. We shouldn't be waiting to get to Heaven to witness the awesome river which flows from God's throne, but we should be accessing and utilizing the precious and powerful river of living water of the Spirit living inside of us.

City of Pure Gold

"... and the city was pure gold, like unto clear glass."
Revelation 21: 18

God calls His Church a city and not just any city, but one of pure gold. And not just any gold, but gold so pure, it's clear as glass. The Body of Christ is a city because cities have city limits, governments, attractions, schools, businesses, agriculture, banks, and families. The five-fold ministry of apostles, prophets, evangelists, pastors, and teachers make up God's government in the Church (***Ephesians 4:11-15***) with Christ as the Mayor. The Body of Christ's city limits stop at the flesh. We walk in the Spirit and not after the flesh (***Galatians 5:16***). The main attraction in the Church is Jesus, the Lamb of God and His work at Calvary. There are many different schools and spiritual places of higher learning in the Church. The Church bank in the Kingdom of God's financial institution is seed time and harvest (***Galatians 8:22***). The Church is a city because others are able to come and visit and if they like what they experience within its city limits, they can decide to take up residence there.

Matthew 5:14 says, "Ye are the light of the world. A city that is set upon a hill cannot be hid." God was not speaking literally of a city, but He was speaking concerning the Bride of Christ. She is the city, the foundation, the streets of Gold, the Pearly Gates. There isn't a city of pure gold waiting for us in Heaven because it was speaking prophetically of God's Church who is filled with the glory of God and walking by faith on streets of Gold.

In my Father's house

Transparency

"And before the throne there was a sea of glass like unto crystal."
Revelation 4:6

One of the most important aspects about God and His Church is the attribute of transparency. *Transparent* means, *transmitting light, able to be seen through with clarity; free of deceit; easily understood or seen through (because of lack of subtlety); admitting the passage of light; open, porous.*[3] Jesus is the Way, the Truth and the Life (*John 14:6*). The Holy Spirit is called the Spirit of Truth (*John 15:26*). God is Truth and His Word is called the Word of Truth. *Truth* simply means, not concealing.[4] Jesus said that there is no truth in satan because he is a liar, deceiver, thief, and surplanter. One of the hallmark qualities of a Christian is the level of truth in which a Christian walks. The Christian life should be a transparent life. Others should not have to guess about our habits or integrity. The more honest a person becomes, the more joy will exude from their life. We are to tell the truth at all times. There is never a reason to not tell the truth, even when it hurts.

32

Our lives should be so clear of the darkness of secret sins and deception, that God's Light should be easily transmitting through us and able to be seen with clarity. It is common place in this generation to befriend someone for many years only to find out later on, that they were not the person you thought they were. This occurs because people live lies. People lie about their education, their financial status, whom they know, their relationship with God and the list goes on and on. The True Church of God is a city of light that's set upon a hill. We cannot transmit light if we are not walking in the light. Before God's Throne was a sea of glass, like a crystal. The sea always represents people of all nations. Before God's Throne was the Redeemed of the Lord from every nation, kindred, people and tongue on Earth (***Revelation 7:9***). This sea is like glass because those before Him are being washed in the Blood of Jesus and have no sin or unclean thing in them. They are transparent, holy, and righteous.

"Having the glory of God: and her light was like unto a stone most precious, even like a jasper stone, clear as crystal."
Revelation 21: 11

Every Believer in Christ is supposed to be clothed with God's Glory. It's His Glory that we wear when we live lives of truth and transparency. When Adam and Eve sinned, they immediately lost God's Glory. We can be gifted and anointed and still live mediocre, Christian lives. But in order to carry God's Glory, it requires not only discipline, but a life of total transparency before God and man. The streets of the New Jerusalem are described as transparent gold because it represents the God-directed, honest, and holy walk of the people of God.

One of the definitions of the word *holy* means *fully integrated with oneself.* In other words, one says what they mean and one means what they say. If people really meant what they said and said what they meant, life would not be as stressful. If our actions paralleled our words, this world would be a different place. Our relationships would be a thousand times better, if the level of transparency in these relationships were greater. If we could totally trust and depend on one another, life would be a lot easier. The Church is pictured as a city of pure, transparent gold because the Church is supposed to be God-directed and living in truth at all times.

Pearly Gates

"And the twelve gates were twelve pearls . . ."
Revelation 21: 21

As aforementioned, the entire 21st chapter of Revelation is not about how Heaven looks, but it's a prophetic picture of the Body of Christ, the Lamb's Bride. Now that we understand this, that means the pearly gates are also a description of the Church and not what is waiting for us in Heaven. To better understand why the Spirit of God chose to describe the Church's gates as pearls, we must continue to allow the Bible to interpret the Bible. Pearls represent Truth. In Jesus' *Parable of the Merchant*, He said that the merchant found a pearl of great price. Then he went and sold all he had to buy the field in which the pearl was located. Proverbs 23:23 says, "Buy the truth and sell it not." In order to obtain truth, it will be expensive, especially the truth of salvation. Salvation is free but it cost God His only begotten Son. When we come to the knowledge of God's salvation and accept it, we pay the price of turning from our old sinful way of living in order to obtain and abide in the great pearl of truth of salvation. The great pearl of salvation is free, but it will cost you everything to walk with Christ. The standard of discipleship is giving everything for the Kingdom of God. Jesus' twelve disciples left everything to walk with Him. Jesus told the rich young ruler to sell everything he had and follow Him. The first Church in the book of Acts sold all their possessions and laid the money at the Apostles feet so that it may be distributed as each one needed.

The New Jerusalem of the Church has twelve gates of pearls because a gate is the place of entrance and pearls represents truth. Therefore, the only way to enter the Body of Christ is by and through truth. We must realize the truth of our sinfulness and the need of a Savior. We must come to grips with the truth that it should have been us on the Cross instead of Jesus and He is our atonement, substitute, and propitiation (Romans 3:25). The truth that there is only one Name under Heaven whereby men shall be saved and that Name is Jesus (Acts 4:12). The truth that Jesus is the Way, the Truth and the Life and no man can come unto the Father except by Him (John 14:6). The gates of the Church are pearls because pearls represent truth and until we know the truth, we will not be free.

3

THE RAPTURE

"Then shall two be in the field; the one shall be taken, and the other left.

Two women shall be grinding at the mill; the one shall be taken, and the other left."

Matthew 24:40-41

This passage is one of the most familiar in the Bible and we have been taught is referring to the *Rapture of the Church*. The word *Rapture* is not in the Bible. The word came from a letter written by one of the Church Fathers. His letter was written in Latin and he used the Latin word *rapturo* which is the translation of the Greek verb *caught up*.[4] The Bible says that the people of God would be *"caught up,"* (*1Thessalonians 4:17*) and the word *Rapture* has the same meaning. Bible teachers have taught for years that this passage is an example of what will happen when Christ comes back for His Church. The apocalyptic book and movie series *Left Behind* comes from this Scripture in **Matthew 24:40-41.** Two will be in the field on the day that Christ returns and one will be left behind. Two women will be grinding at a mill when Christ returns and one will be left behind. What none of the teachers or Bible scholars ever mention is the fact that none of it is true. Ninety percent of the end time prophecy teaching concerning the rapture of the Church and the Tribulation Period is totally misinterpreted and it is not true. As we go through each passage, the truth will be so clear; we will wonder how we ever got it wrong. We are covering the *Doctrine of the Rapture* because the *Rapture* is the supernatural means by which the Church is supposed to meet Jesus and proceed to Heaven.

The first thing we need to understand about the **Matthew 24** teaching of being "left behind" is that Jesus was not talking about the Church because the Church had not been established yet. The Church did not exist until after Christ's resurrection. This is why Pentecost is the birthday of the Church. The Lord would not have been talking about something His disciples had no knowledge of at the time. The disciples asked Jesus what would happen at the end of the age. Jesus was speaking concerning the nation of Israel, not the Church. They did not ask Him what would happen to the Church. If Christ was speaking about the Church in this passage, Paul would not have had these words to say in *1 Corinthians 15:51-52*.

"Behold, I show you a mystery; we shall not all sleep, but we shall all be changed.

In a moment, in the twinkling of an eye, at the last trump: for the trumpet shall sound, and the dead shall be raised incorruptible, and we shall be changed."

If Jesus was teaching about the *Rapture of the Church* in the *Matthew 24* discourse, Paul would not have referred to the same event as a mystery. A mystery is something that is hidden or a secret. If Jesus was speaking concerning the *Rapture,* and later on Paul is revealing a mystery, which was the "catching away" of the Church, this would be a great contradiction. The truth is, Jesus was not talking about the *Rapture of the Church. Matthew 24:3* says,

"And as he sat upon the Mount of Olives, the disciples came unto him privately, saying, tell us, when shall these things be? And what shall be the sign of thy coming, and of the end of the world?"

Jesus' conversation had to do with the end of the age and His Second Coming. When Jesus said, "...two be in the field; the one shall be taken and the other left," many have understood that to refer to either the *Rapture* or the "catching away" of the 144,000 Jewish Believers left on Earth to evangelize during the Great Tribulation Period. But neither conclusion is accurate. In Luke's Gospel, he records Jesus' discourse of the signs of the end of the age (the same as the **Matthew 24** discourse) but he adds something that helps bring illumination.

Judgment of the Wicked

"Where the carcasses are, the eagles would be gathered."
Matthew 24:28

*T*he one taken out the field and the one taken from the grinding mill are those taken for judgment and death, not the Christian. They are those who are instantly judged and their dead bodies are heaped together for the birds of prey to devour. Eagles are known for eating dead carcasses, but the translators used eagles when it is literally translated vultures.[5] ***Revelation 19:17-18*** explains it better.

"And I saw an angel standing in the sun; and he cried with a loud voice, saying to all the fowls that fly in the midst of heaven. Come and gather yourselves together unto the supper of the great God.

That ye may eat the flesh of kings, and the flesh of captains and the flesh of mighty men, and the flesh of horses, and of them that sit on them, and the flesh of all men, both free and bond, both small and great."

Anytime God judged and destroyed a nation or nations, He protected the righteous before dealing with the wicked. God is not Someone who runs from a fight. He not only protects what is His, what is His remains while the wicked are taken away. The "two be in the field" that Jesus taught about, was a picture of *The Parable of Wheat and Tares.* During harvest time, it is the tares that is taken and burned while the wheat remained. The one that is taken in the field and the one taken from the grinding mill are the wicked. It is the righteous person who was not taken because the meek shall inherit the Earth, they shall not be taken from it.

As the Days of Noah

"But as the days of Noe were, so shall also the coming of the Son of man be.

For as in the day that were before the flood they were eating and drinking, marrying and giving in marriage, until the day that Noe entered into the ark,

And knew not until the flood came, and took them all away; so shall also the coming of the Son of man be."

Matthew 24:37-39

It was this passage that preceded Jesus' teaching on *the two in the field* and *the two at the mill* in verses 40-41. During the days of Noah, before God judged the Earth with the flood, the message of salvation was preached by Noah for 120 years. Noah told them that the ark was their only way of escape and that a great rain was coming to destroy the Earth. The people continued in their day to day living, throwing caution to the wind. Jesus said that if the homeowner knew the day the thief would break in, he would have been prepared. (**Matthew 24:43**). Jesus is never considered a thief to the righteous. The righteous look forward to His arrival. It is the unrighteous that will see Him as a thief because He is coming when they least expect it, to take away the sinful lifestyle to which they have become accustomed.

Noah and his family never left the Earth. God did not remove them. In the end they were the ones who remained. We have to get past this mentality that the devil is going to one day take over God's planet and God will rush and get His people out of harms' way so that the anti-Christ will not kill them. The truth is, it will be God doing the harming and it will be the wicked doing the running. **Revelation 6:15-17** explains,

"And the kings of the earth, and the great men, and the rich men, and the chief captains, and the mighty men, and every bondman, and every free man, hid themselves in the dens and in the rocks of the mountains.

And said to the mountains and rocks, Fall on us, and hide us from the face of him that sitteth on the throne, and from the wrath of the Lamb:

For the great day of his wrath is come; and who shall be able to stand?"

Noah's day reveals how the wicked was removed and the righteous remained. Sodom and Gomorrah shows us evil men being judged and removed and righteous Lot and his daughters remained. There is such a spirit of escapism in the Church today that it's amazing that anyone would want to follow the God we say we serve. Jesus never once told us to prepare to leave the Earth that God gave us dominion over. The entire purpose of Christ coming in the flesh was to restore the dominion we once had before The Fall. Why would He go through all He went through just to have us in a constant state of emergency because the devil is going to take over God's planet soon? We are so consumed with His Coming that we are missing His Presence. Let's look at Jesus' own words concerning removing the righteous from the Earth.

"I pray not that thou shouldest take them out of the world, but that thou shouldest keep them from the evil."

John 17:15

God is not a Landlord that plans on returning to evict the good paying tenants from their residence and allowing the bad tenants to take over his real estate. He is the kind of Landlord that will return like a thief in the night to evict the bad tenants while giving the good tenants more real estate for being faithful.

We are taught about all the power and authority the Believer has in Christ. We boldly declare about the Armor of God we wear, the name of Jesus, the anointing of the Holy Ghost, the gifts and fruit of the Spirit, the Word of God, the Angels on assignment for us. We preach about how the devil is afraid of us because of the wealth of power at the Church's disposal and how we are ready for war, yet when it is time for the big throw down at the end of the age we believe God will snatch us away before we can get in the fight!

Jesus did not instruct us to be preoccupied with His coming, but to occupy until He comes. The matter is not His coming because He already told us He's coming, but the real matter is His presence; His presence in our lives right now to manifest Heaven on Earth and establish His Kingdom.

4

HEAVEN'S REWARD

"But as it is written, Eye hath not seen, nor ear heard, neither have entered into the heart of man, the things which God hath prepared for them that love him."

1 Corinthians 2:9

Heaven is such an awesome place, dimension, and state of mind, that it's one of those instances where we are going to just have to be there to believe it. How can we describe infinity? How can we articulate perfection? Outside of a few passages where men of God had visions of God's throne, there is very little written in the Bible concerning Heaven. God designed it this way because He plans on literally "blowing our minds" when we make it there. Apostle Paul gives us a firsthand account of this in *2 Corinthians 12:2,4,*

"I knew a man in Christ above fourteen years ago, (whether in the body, I cannot tell; or whether out of the body, I cannot tell: God knoweth;) such an one caught up to the third heaven.

47

How that he was caught up into paradise, and heard unspeakable words, which it is not lawful for a man to utter."

Paul had a visit to Heaven and admitted the things he heard were unspeakable and not lawful to repeat. If what he heard had this effect, imagine the reality of what he saw. If the Christians that truly love Christ and live faithful lives on Earth, enduring life's sufferings, persecutions, trials, and heartaches, only have a mansion to look forward to in Heaven, they would be very disappointed. I do not believe we are even capable of imagining Heavenly things because we are so used to Earthly things. Our eyes truly have not seen and our ears truly have not heard the things God has prepared for us.

Rewards

*T*he Word of God has much to say concerning the rewards that faithful Believers will receive for living for Christ. God loves rewarding His people for all of their hard work, honest lives, and integrity. Here are just a few Scriptures detailing this promise.

"And, behold, I come quickly, and my reward is with me, to give every man according as his work shall be."

Revelation 22:12

"For the Son of man shall come in the glory of his Father with his angels; and then he shall reward every man according to his works."

Matthew 16:27

"Rejoice ye in that day, and leap for joy: for, behold, your reward is great in heaven…"

Luke 6:23

"But love ye your enemies, and do good, and lend, hoping for noting again; and your reward shall be great, and ye shall be the children of the Highest…"

Luke 6:35

In my Father's house

"**Knowing that of the Lord ye shall receive the reward of the inheritance: for ye serve the Lord Christ.**"

Colossians 3:24

"**. . . he is a rewarder of them that diligently seek him.**"

Hebrews 11:6

"**Look to yourselves, that we lose not those things which we have wrought, but that we receive a full reward.**"

2 John 1:8

Crowns

G od did not go into detail about what kind of reward we would receive in Heaven. But I am sure it's because it simply cannot be explained in the dimension of this fallen world that we live in now. The Bible also speaks about crowns that the righteous will receive from God for obeying His commandments in this life. God saves every tear we shed (*Psalm 42:3*) and He remembers every sacrifice we make for the cause of Christ. Each time we feed the hungry, clothe the naked, visit the prisoners, take care of the fatherless and widow, walk in unconditional love, crucify the flesh, obey the leading of the Holy Ghost, and invest in Kingdom business, God records it all and is waiting for the season where He can bless us and give us our reward and our crowns. These rewards are on top of the fact that we will receive eternal life, no more sickness, disease or death. We will not be limited by time and space. Our ultimate reward will be meeting our Savior, and Father God. Here are just a few Scriptures concerning the crowns He has for us.

"Behold, I come quickly: hold that fast which thou hast, that no man take thy crown."

Revelation 3:11

"And when the chief Shepherd shall appear, ye shall receive a crown of glory that fadeth not away."

1 Peter 5:4

"Blessed is the man that endureth temptation; for when he is tried, he shall receive the crown of life, which the Lord hath promised to them that love him."

James 1:12

"And every man that striveth for the mastery is temperate in all things. Now they do it to obtain a corruptible crown; but we an incorruptible."

1 Corinthians 9:25

In the New Testament, there are four crowns given to Believers by the Lord Jesus Christ. Each crown is unique and each crown is a reward. First, there is the *crown of rejoicing* found in **1 Thessalonians 2:19**. Those people that we lead to the Lord and/or disciple become a crown to us. Secondly, there is the *crown of righteousness*. (**2Timothy 4:7-8**) This is a crown that we will receive for keeping the faith and for loving His appearing. Next, is the *crown of life* found in **James 1:12** *and* **Revelation**

2:10. This is a crown that we will receive for not giving into temptation and for enduring tribulation (faithfulness.) And lastly, is the *crown of glory*. This is a crown that pastors and elders will receive for willingly feeding the flock out of a pure heart with pure motives. These pastors and elders are also good examples to the Body of Christ that God has given them to oversee. (*1Peter 5:1-4*)

The Universe

Many Bible scholars and scientists have speculated that the size and enormity of the universe must have some purpose to it in the scheme of God's overall plan. As we examine how everything God makes has a specific purpose, it is easy to look at one of His most magnificent creations (the Universe) and ask the question; what purpose does it serve? What purpose does trillions of stars and billions of solar systems have? I believe the creation of Adam, God's first man, was just the beginning of a much larger purpose. God intended for Adam to rule and have dominion over planet Earth. He may intend for the rest of the planets and solar systems to be inhabited, as well. We have very little insight into this plan because it was cut short with Adam's fall. I believe if Adam had been faithful with his stewardship over Earth, other planets would have been granted for his seed to rule.

What if our reward for enduring the hardships of this life was our own galaxy? What if God gave you your own planet, moon, sun, and stars? What if the billions of empty, uninhabited, beautiful galaxies were waiting just for the redeemed of the Lord? I do not believe Angels are working like slaves in Heaven right now just to build us a nice mansion for our faithfulness here on Earth. I believe God has plans to literally "blow our minds," and inheriting part of this vast universe would do exactly that. Do not be too upset that Heaven may not have streets of gold, or pearly gates, or be filled with mansions. We should be so excited that what God has in store for the Saints is beyond what we could ever ask or think!

Prayer of Salvation

Heavenly Father, I come to you admitting that I am a sinner. I choose to turn away from sin, and I ask You to cleanse me of all unrighteousness. I believe your Son, Jesus, died so that I may be forgiven of my sins and made righteous through faith in Him. I call upon the Name of Jesus Christ to be my Savior and the Lord of my life. Jesus, I choose to follow You and I ask that You fill me with the power of the Holy Spirit. I declare I am a child of God. I am free from sin and full of the righteousness of God. I am saved. In Jesus' Name. **Amen**.

About the Author

Romel Duane Moore Sr. was born in Chicago, Illinois. He served as Pastor of Liberty Temple Full Gospel Church of Fort Wayne, Indiana for five years. Moore has worked in middle schools, group homes, and has served as Director of a Faith-Based Program Unity of Love Family Reconnect, helping inmates readjust after being released from prison. He has worked closely with re-entry court programs, serving as a liaison between ex-offenders and re-entry court. Moore has taught in prisons and juvenile facilities in Illinois, Indiana, Ohio, Georgia, and Florida. He is a mentor with Big Brothers, Big Sisters and the Boys and Girls Clubs of America. Moore actively volunteers with Red Cross. He holds crusades, feeds the homeless, and cares for the helpless. He is a twenty-year Accounting professional. Romel's books are available on Amazon, Kindle and Createspace. If you desire to have Romel speak at an event you can reach him at (808) 397-4906.

Footnotes

[1]The New Strong's Expanded Exhaustive Concordance of the Bible, Copyright © 2001 by Thomas Nelson Publishers. Published in Nashville, TN, by Thomas Nelson, Inc. Greek word #3438.

[2]Ibid.

[3] The New Strong's Expanded Exhaustive Concordance of the Bible, Copyright © 2001 by Thomas Nelson Publishers. Published in Nashville, TN, by Thomas Nelson, Inc. Greek word for manifold #4182 *polupoikilos* means *much variegated, multifarious* and *manifold;* from #4183 and from the Greek word #4164 *poikilos* meaning *particolored; variegated,* and *divers.* Manifold wisdom is found in Ephesians 3:10.

[4]American Heritage Dictionary.

[5] Ibid.

[6]https://bible.org; *Where did the term 'rapture' come from?* This article was published on January 1, 2001.

[7] The New Strong's Expanded Exhaustive Concordance of the Bible, Copyright © 2001 by Thomas Nelson Publishers. Published in Nashville, TN, by Thomas Nelson, Inc. Greek word #105.

Made in the USA
Middletown, DE
22 October 2024